How to *Really* *Love* Your Job

DON OSGOOD

POCKET GUIDE ™
Tyndale House Publishers, Inc.
Wheaton, Illinois

Adapted from *Breaking Through* by Don Osgood, copyright © 1986 by Don Osgood

"How to Retire at Thirty-five" adapted from an advertisement created by Marstellar (now HCM), 866 Third Ave., New York, N.Y. 10022.

Pocket Guide is a trademark of Tyndale House Publishers, Inc.

Library of Congress Card Catalog 90-70994
ISBN 0-8423-2830-0

97 96 95 94 93 92 91 90
10 9   8   7   6   5   4   3   2   1

CONTENTS

Take Charge of Your Job!

To every problem there is already a solution whether you know it or not.—
Grenville Kleiser

Has your job become a silent prison, holding you trapped in circumstances that sap your motivation and commitment to work?

Perhaps the walls of your prison were built quietly, steadily, as you first welcomed the security of a regular paycheck, relaxed in the comfort of company benefits, or received salary increases that encouraged you. Maybe you were rocketed to levels you never expected. But suddenly one day you began to wonder: *What is this all for? Why do I feel frustrated about my work? Is there a better job for me somewhere else? Will a good paycheck guarantee happiness?*

BREAKING OUT OF THE WORK RUT

If you feel this way, you are not alone. There is a solution for you. But first, you've got to want to take charge of your job and your career.

I broke out of a routine attitude and learned to be the leader of my job. I'd like to show you how to do the same, just as I have for such organizations as IBM, DuPont, and Continental Insurance Company. Employees from these companies have become leaders in their jobs, utilizing the ideas in this book. Like them, you can become a leader on your job, either changing it so that you can love it or building a road from it to a job that you can love.

In thirty years at IBM, trying a lot of positions, I finally figured out how to change the one I was already in. I re-created the last five jobs and loved every one of them. Then I left to start my own business, and now I love the business I've created.

Along the way, I've learned an important secret: Don't accept anyone's definition or description of your job or career. Most job definitions are attempts to satisfy salary administrators. And all job descriptions are out of date as soon as a leader occupies the job, especially if the leader occupies it with an eye to what's behind it.

In this book you'll learn how to think of the purpose of your job—the real one, not the one in your job description. We'll look at what I call "power" questions—questions necessary to discover what the real job *should* be. And we'll discover the four rooms or opportunities to explore in every job, including yours. We'll also discover how seven attitudes can make or break your career, how four new steps in motivation can make you a more creative and decisive person, and how to best deal with your manager to get more freedom in your work.

But first, we need to look more closely at an innovative leadership approach that will work for you.

DECIDING TO
TAKE A NEW APPROACH

Ever notice how some people seem to greet their jobs almost the way you greet an exhilarating morning at the beach or the fresh powder on a sunny ski slope or the sunset over a clean trout stream? Often the difference between them and others is their approach.

As I write these words while traveling on a train from Washington to New York, the conductor is literally changing his job, which is otherwise terribly routine. His voice on the loudspeaker has announced each station with originality—coaxing once, encouraging next, joshing now, and always conveying vitality. I have been listening carefully as he has carried out what must be a very precise job description of what he is to say at every station. But he has said the words his way, with his own planned hesitation and emphasis.

"Station stop . . . New-ark, New Jer-sey!" he says, as though New Jersey is the

Garden of Eden and Newark is the fountain of youth. "It's Newark, folks!" he exclaims triumphantly. Then his pitch drops with an added hint of the sinister. "Watch . . . your . . . step."

This conductor is performing his job to the letter, but he brings something special to it. His interpretation. Himself.

You can bring a new approach, a personal creativity, and an authority to your job just as this conductor did.

BECOMING THE PRESIDENT OF YOUR JOB

Think big for a moment. Assume you are the president of the United States. What authority would you have the opportunity to exercise, considering the many precedents about what a president does or does not do?

I had the chance to examine one real president's approach to his job through the insight of a former secretary of the army, the late Frank Pace. Pace used to tell me about Harry Truman, a man who many saw as unsophisticated and unprepared for the presidency when he assumed the office.

I had not thought about Truman as a great leader. But as Frank Pace described how Truman approached the presidency, I developed a deep respect for this common man who changed the course of history. He brought one key quality to his work that all of us can foster: decisiveness about his job. He managed his job rather than letting his job manage him.

According to Pace, Truman, who grew up on a farm and whose highest rank in World War I had been a captain, took the helm of the presidency without hesitation. He was not awed by his job description or intimidated by the history of the job. Instead, as pages 10-11 show, he demonstrated a take-charge attitude, the same attitude he showed when a haberdashery he co-owned failed during the Great Depression, and, rather than go into bankruptcy, he chose to pay off the debt over a ten-year period.

Like Truman, you can overcome your lack of experience, your circumstances, even your job description. Just as Harry Truman took authority and made key decisions in his job, so you can make key decisions in your job—decisions that will affect your future and the futures of those around you.

You can become the president of your job. But it will require a take-charge attitude on your part.

☞ The Nine Decisions of Harry Truman

You can make key decisions *within the description of your present job* as Harry Truman did when he assumed the presidency. Here, for example, are the nine most important decisions of Harry Truman as seen through the eyes of Frank Pace.

1. He decided how to terminate the war in Japan. In guiding him on this first and one of the most substantial challenges of his career, his joint chiefs of staff recommended invasion. "How many American lives would it cost?" asked Mr. Truman. The answer: "300,000 to 400,000." "How many Japanese lives?" The answer came back: "Over a million." "That," said Mr. Truman, "is not acceptable." He based the decision to use the atom bomb on its minimal impact on life and property.

2. He chose to give the defeated enemy considerate treatment after World War II. (This action ran so contrary to Joseph Stalin's nature that some effective persuasion had to come into play. Knowing Stalin's dislike for Winston Churchill, Frank Pace asserts that President Truman played the effective middleman and achieved the desired results.)

3. Truman decided to preserve Berlin by airlift rather than attacking along

the corridor. (When the Allied powers occupied Germany, Russia enveloped Berlin, leaving the United States without access by land to the city, even though all the Allies were to occupy Berlin.) Frank Pace states that the wisdom of this choice has never been challenged.

4. The president decided to establish a boundary of United States support for Greece and Turkey against Russian incursion, preserving the existence of those two nations.

5. Truman supported the creation of NATO, with all its implications for preserving peace in Europe over forty years, and made Europe a major link in free-world defense.

6. President Truman signed the legislation that put the Marshall Plan into effect, insuring the economic solvency of Europe after World War II.

7. Truman supported the controversial creation of the state of Israel when it became apparent that a home for the Jewish people had to be established.

8. He decided to bring the United States into the Korean War. One week later the United Nations voted to send its forces into the conflict.

9. Truman chose not to use the atom bomb when our soldiers were being threatened by overwhelming Chinese forces during the Korean War.

YOU CAN BE A LEADER

Becoming the leader of your job is another way of saying you can take charge of your career—and ultimately take more responsibility for your approach to life. Unless you invest *yourself* into the decisions about your career, job, and life, consciously applying your total purpose to them, someone else will make your decisions for you based on their needs alone.

One of the most common mistakes of people at work is to assume that the boss knows more than they do about what the job should be. If you have been in your job long enough to know what it should be, or might become, you have the opportunity and the responsibility as a leader to remake it.

Leadership isn't what most people think it is. In the thousands of books that have been written about the topic, we have tended to overlook how leadership starts. Many times we don't even think about leadership beyond the supervisory or managerial level. But what if we did? What would an attitude of leadership at any level of the job hierarchy do for an individual's vitality and job satisfaction, not to mention productivity?

In 1967 I asked some representatives of the Southern Christian Leadership Conference (SCLC) to define *leadership* for me since their organization name included the word and since their president, Dr. Martin

Luther King, Jr., had shown the world that he was a leader.

Subsequently, one of Dr. King's staff persons addressed the IBM management class I conducted at the time. He was bright, articulate, and enthusiastic. When I introduced Andrew Young to the group of managers, no one recognized his name, but that day we listened to the future ambassador to the United Nations and mayor of Atlanta. Instead of defining leadership, he described in strikingly simple and reasonable terms how SCLC selected leaders.

"When we go into a town where we feel there is racial injustice," he said, "we ask the first of three questions: 'Who in this town thinks there is a problem?' When we find a group of people who think there is a problem, we ask, 'Who thinks something ought to be done about this problem?' To those who respond, we ask the third question, 'Do *you* want to do something about the problem?' Those who do are the group from which we find our leaders."

I have never forgotten that description because I've found it works for any organization and any individual. It enables you and me to recognize, create, and utilize the productivity within ourselves whether or not we are called leaders.

To review, leadership occurs when someone:

- knows something needs to be done
- has an idea of what he or she ought to do
- does something about it

When you apply these three simple yet profound steps to your specific job and organization, professional leadership occurs—with commensurate job satisfaction. It *always* occurs. Few people have recognized this unwritten law!

There is nothing magical or uncommon about leadership. Anyone can acquire it in any walk of life and in any organization. You can be a leader in your job by looking at yourself and your approach to your work in a new way. And the results will move you that much closer to really loving your job.

Are you ready to approach your job with authority, with decisiveness, with innovative leadership? If so, you have just embarked on *the* venture that can set you free from the prison of your job. To help you get started, we will now consider the seven attitudes I mentioned before—attitudes that set the stage for your new approach to your job.

Seven Attitudes That Make or Break You

The greatest discovery of our generation is that a human being can alter his life by altering his attitudes.—William James

Have you ever heard someone say, "He's always tripping over his ego" or, "She's like an uncoiled spring. There's no ambition left"?

These comments indicate that the person in question holds one of seven basic attitudes shown on page 16. All people have each of these attitudes at some time in their lives. Some of the attitudes are positive. Some are not.

These attitudes show up in careers, marriages, and personal experiences. The order in which they appear is not always the same for each person. But in one way or another, they have a marked effect on everything a person does. They spell the difference between productivity and inactivity, between fruitful friendship and loss of friendship, between success and failure, between loving your job and merely marking time in it.

Take Ralph Kennedy (not his real name), for instance. Ralph attended an IBM leadership school I ran, later called New Perspectives. At fifty, Ralph had resigned himself to work as an instructor at an education facility until retirement. Within several months of leaving the school, he had negotiated a different job and ended up working in the White House in a marketing job he really loved. And it all began with a change in attitudes.

Contrary to widespread opinion, it is never too late to change your attitude and to set your career or, for that matter, your personal life back on course. We'll see how Ralph did it and how you can do it, too. The first step is to become more aware of your attitudes.

1. Idealistic 7. Committed
2. Frustrated 6. Decisive
3. Defiant 5. Aware
4. Resigned

Chart 1

IDEALISTIC
The idealistic attitude is a "new beginning" attitude, marked by high hopes and enthusiasm. Such an attitude occurs with the onset of your career or a major change in your job or life, such as marriage. People with this attitude feel they can make virtu-

ally anything work out well because they have the right talents and are in the right place at the right time.

FRUSTRATED

When a person begins to see a gap between personal expectations or desires and present circumstances, worry or anxiety sets in and momentum slows down. A person may ask, *What's really going on here? Where am I heading?*

This is a time of troublesome indecision brought about by a fear that things may not work out as well as expected. Sustained frustration (often from fear and indecision) brings on anxiety, and that is never motivating or productive for an organization, marriage, or an individual. Frustration becomes the breeding ground for the next attitude.

DEFIANT

After experiencing frustration, a person comes to a conclusion that things clearly won't work out as expected unless something definite is done. Often this happens when a person sees a wide gap between personal expectations and reality or when a long time goes by with no change in a positive direction.

When the defiant attitude occurs, fear and indecision are no longer forces. A reactive attitude replaces them, an attitude that says in essence, "I guess I'm going to

☞ Ten Laws about Attitudes

1. There is nothing uncommon or mysterious about an attitude. Everyone has attitudes, and everyone can learn how to deal with them.

2. Anyone can create an attitude in himself or herself.

3. Anyone can prevent or change his or her attitude.

4. Whenever two or more people are involved, the attitudes of one ultimately will affect the other. The attitudes of both eventually will affect the organization.

5. New attitudes and changes in old attitudes are a product of a gap between:

   - *Expectations*—what you expected in the past.
   - *Reality*—what you find happening now.
   - *Desire*—what you really want to happen in the future.

have to make some changes here if no one else will." Now defiance or anger sets in.

There are two levels of defiance: covert and overt. Neither is constructive, but covert defiance proves especially unproductive—even destructive—in the long run. A covert-defiant person often doesn't know that he or she is defiant and may bury personal anger for days, months, even years. Longer service employees or people married for a long time may have this atti-

6. The size of the gap and the intensity of your desire to change the gap will determine both your specific attitude right now and the speed with which your attitude changes.

7. Your attitude affects both your leadership ability as an individual and the leadership position of your organization, whether it is an athletic team, business, church, government, or your family.

8. Your attitude changes are ultimately noticeable by the general public.

9. Knowledge about your attitudes is not the privileged domain of specialists but your own responsibility and privilege.

10. Because your attitudes are invisibly created within, often long before anyone can see the results on the outside, you can discern your attitudes in yourself and similar attitudes in others long before they result in actions.

tude for many years without realizing it. This buried defiance can lead to attitude number four, *resigned*.

RESIGNED

The resigned attitude occurs when a person feels there is no longer any use in trying to change things. Often people mentally resign from their jobs or from some other commitment, such as a marriage, but they don't actually leave. Their bodies are still around, but their creative, productive spark is gone.

Such people will do what is legally or socially required and little more. They stop trying to make constructive contributions and move to a more passive role. They become people who hang on or hang around saying, "What's the use?" Usually only major effort by someone else will cause change in the resigned person.

Those who have acquired a "What's the use?" attitude engage in a form of pouting or vindictiveness. There are several symptoms of this: a sudden preference for working or being alone, missed schedules or appointments, a pattern of unaccountable absence, increased drinking, irritability, or faultfinding.

The resigned attitude is always serious, not only for the person who has it but also for others. It can become contagious, but the next attitude can help.

AWARE
People reach an attitude of awareness when they see they must be willing to change. They accept personal responsibility and the need to initiate personal change.

Someone else's honesty often causes awareness. Sometimes, for example, an individual can be brought to awareness by a statement about the real situation. A supervisor might say to an employee, "Ann, I'm worried about you. I feel that you are drifting, and I'm afraid of what this may lead to in a few months."

There is always a risk here for a person who makes such a comment. Such honesty isn't always wanted! But often a constructive, straightforward approach can lead to a helpful discussion if the person starting the discussion couples his comments with real concern.

We bring on the awareness attitude ourselves when we look squarely in the mirror and accept ourselves for who we are—or someone else for who he or she is. In taking stock of ourselves, we recognize the possibility that nothing good will come unless change takes place. In a moment we will see how straightforward "power" questions can bring awareness.

Awareness sets the stage for the next attitude. With awareness, nothing can stop decisiveness from coming on like a refreshing rain—or a tidal wave of constructive activity.

DECISIVE
This is an active, productive attitude. While awareness triggers decisiveness, it doesn't occur until change is actually begun—until you pull the trigger.

As you take any new step, decision is born—while your foot is in the air. This exhilarating, stress-releasing attitude starts in your heart, transfers to your head, and ends in your feet and your hands.

Decisive people *consciously* do something different. Sometimes you must learn to take an entirely new step, especially if you've become too comfortable for your own good. Sometimes it is necessary to decide to do something different in a safer, smaller area of life or work before tackling a main area.

All of us want to be decisive unless we've been hurt too much or too often. For most people, being decisive brings freedom. For some it is like breaking out of prison. For organizations it is the breath of vitality that pumps new vigor into the work that needs doing. But one more attitude sustains the vitality that decisiveness starts. It's called "commitment," and it's an essential part of success.

COMMITTED

We become committed when we don't expect perfection of our organization, our marriage, our relationship, or even ourselves, yet we want to make things work. We strive for excellence, knowing that perfection is often idealistic.

The committed attitude is not a reaction to things that are going wrong but an active, working desire to help out. There is no idealistic feeling in this attitude. No magic words guarantee that everything will turn out all right. Rather, there is a practical understanding that we must work together—with imperfect people. Jobs become workable and relationships become productive when we get the stars out of our eyes, put our shoulders to work, and push on toward our goals.

YOUR ATTITUDE INVENTORY

Now that you have examined these seven attitudes, you are ready to discover which of them apply to you.

Use the three barometers below and on the following page. Ask yourself, *Which attitude best describes me right now? In each of these areas, what attitude have I had during the last twelve months?* Then check your responses on each curve.

Discuss your answers with someone who knows you and will disagree with you if he or she feels differently from you about your attitudes. This will give you a greater appreciation of reality. Next, draw an arrow on each attitude curve to the attitude you want.

MY ATTITUDE ON THE JOB

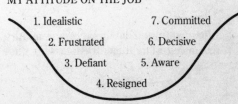

1. Idealistic   7. Committed

2. Frustrated   6. Decisive

3. Defiant   5. Aware

4. Resigned

Chart 2

MY ATTITUDE IN MY FAMILY

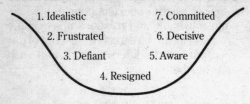

1. Idealistic	7. Committed
2. Frustrated	6. Decisive
3. Defiant	5. Aware
4. Resigned	

Chart 3

MY ATTITUDE IN MY PERSONAL LIFE

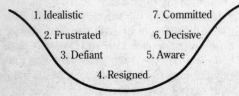

1. Idealistic	7. Committed
2. Frustrated	6. Decisive
3. Defiant	5. Aware
4. Resigned	

Chart 4

There are many shapes to your career, marriage, or personal life over time. With long years of experience, your curve can look like the one below.

With extended resignation or apathy, your curve can look like the following illustration.

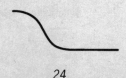

For some, the curve will look like this one.

Any major change in life such as a new job, a physical move, or marriage can set your attitude curve back to attitude number one, idealistic.

Now think of the impact of your attitude on others in your organization or your family. Your attitude affects others. It influences your ability to communicate with them. And that can change your future. Your attitude will make or break not only you but also those around you!

CREATING NEW ATTITUDES

Remember Ralph Kennedy, the man who attained a job in the White House after attending a leadership school? Ralph's new attitudes toward his work started with straightforward questions—questions that caused him to move first to awareness, the fifth attitude, and then beyond it to decisiveness and commitment.

I interviewed Ralph while making a videotape on the impact of the professional leadership program he had attended. I asked him if he had felt any dissatisfaction in his former job.

"Yes. Down underneath, when I really thought about it, I wanted something more," he related. "I knew I wouldn't be happy to keep doing what I was doing."

"What did you really want?" I asked.

"I wanted to get back into sales again. I didn't dream I could get the White House job. But my manager listened to me, and I got the job."

"How old were you then, Ralph?"

"Fifty-one."

"Thinking of the seven attitudes, Ralph, tell us how you related to them."

"I had dipped in my attitude. I might have been frustrated or even resigned, but I pulled back up, and now I'm committed."

Ralph explained how he had reviewed his past expectations, looked at his current observations about where he really stood, and discovered his desire for something more. With that awareness came decisiveness and commitment.

PAST EXPECTATIONS

GAP

PRESENT REALITY

GAP

FUTURE DESIRES

Chart 5

As I have talked with people over the years, I have discovered the impact of *defining gaps*—gaps between past expectations, present reality, and future hopes. When these gaps are clearly seen, I have found that attitudes tend to change.

In a diagram, the expectation gaps look like Chart 5.

Like Ralph, you can ask yourself three straightforward questions about the course of your job:

1. What did I expect?
2. What is really happening now that is different from my expectations?
3. What do I really want to happen now that I have determined what is really happening?

Anyone who asks these questions of himself or herself and of others can find the beginnings of attitude change. Use the box on page 29 to help you examine your attitude gaps.

CHECK YOUR ATTITUDE GAPS

When you answer the gap questions we have been discussing, you will likely discover personal gaps. As you explore ways to close them, things start to happen. New vitality will begin as you move from awareness to decisiveness and commitment.

Let's suppose you had high expectations about your job, you have a satisfying feeling about it now, and you have a desire to continue on your present path. You are reaching for yet higher expectations and deeper satisfactions, and you have the desire to see your hopes achieved. If this description fits you, your attitudes are generally positive, life is good, and motivation is normal.

But suppose you had high expectations about your job and few of them worked out. As a result, you really feel dissatisfied. If your desire to try again remains strong, you have already moved from awareness to decisiveness and may well be knocking on the door of commitment.

Of course, you could also go another way: high expectations, low results, discouragement. Or perhaps you began with low expectations and have achieved average success—you haven't failed and you haven't turned your world upside down. Suppose also that you feel content to let things remain as they are; you have little desire for new achievement.

If you or someone you know has reached this place in life, you will discover many others there, too. Individuals with attitudes like these often maintain the functions that every organization has.

But there are some people who have given up. They are the uncoiled springs in life. Still others have burned out. If you feel these descriptions fit you, or someone you know feels they fit you, you will benefit from discovering the secrets of motivation we'll discuss in the next chapter, "Thirty Days to New Motivation."

☞My Attitude Gaps

1. List below your past expectations, assessment of the present, and desires for the future.
2. Determine what changes you can make in your expectations, your present situation, and your future by placing a check mark by the item you could change.
3. Discuss these proposed changes with a trustworthy friend.

For this circumstance . . . (name an important present circumstance)

My past expectations were . . .

My present assessment of the situation is . . .

My desires for the future are . . .

Thirty Days to New Motivation

To survive, men and business and corporations must serve.—John H. Patterson

Every time I think of motivation, I remember the humorous story about the Olympic athlete who was practicing for the shotput competition. I can almost see him now in my mind's eye. As he practiced putting the shot, he backed into the javelin thrower's pointed javelin and won the standing broad jump! Some say that is motivation. Not me. The athlete moved quickly, but he wasn't motivated. He was just reacting.

What is motivation? What produces the commitment we examined in the seven attitudes? What motivates you on the job?

For years Abraham Maslow's hierarchy of needs and Frederick Herzberg's ideas on motivation dominated American thought on what motivates you and me. Maslow identified five developmental levels of need that a person can have satisfied. Each builds upon the last, according to Maslow, and one must be fulfilled before the next level can be reached. They form a pyramid, as shown in Chart 1.

MASLOW'S HIERARCHY

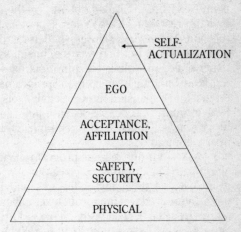

SELF-ACTUALIZATION

EGO

ACCEPTANCE, AFFILIATION

SAFETY, SECURITY

PHYSICAL

Chart 1

Maslow described self-actualization as the ultimate motivation, though he modified this view toward the end of his life. Herzberg, in contrast, emphasized work itself as a motivator. Both brought their heritage of individualism to work and drew on it in writing about motivation. But they focused heavily on self-interest, and there is much more to motivation than that.

THE REST OF THE STORY

Think for a moment beyond self-interest. What happens after people establish themselves in their careers and find self-actualization? Is self-interest the ultimate source of our motivation?

History shows that people through the centuries were motivated not only by their own interests but also by causes, personal mission, discovery, service, beliefs, and creativity itself. In thirty years of business experience, including teaching, counseling, and building management programs on local, national, and international levels, I have found that people reach a point in life when self-interest isn't enough. Not nearly enough.

I worked for one year as program manager for IBM's Community Executive Program. In that time, my colleagues and I taught hundreds of nonprofit executives from the Red Cross, Boy Scouts, Girl Scouts, Heart Association, YMCA, YWCA, United Way, NAACP, and scores of other organizations, representing Latin, Asian, African, and American cultures as well as Jewish and Christian heritages. Most of the executives were drawn into America's multibillion-dollar nonprofit sector by a sense of service as well as self. They were looking for a way to help, not just a way to be helped. They were looking for a worthwhile cause.

Religious motivations have endured, even though impacted by self-serving motives. America was explored not only by self-interested people but also by purpose-motivated Christians and Jews. Why do people give up possessions, birthrights, family life, citizenship, personal freedom, even life itself for causes beyond themselves? Both history and current social action give us evidence of motivation that includes but goes beyond self-interest.

FOUR PURPOSE MOTIVATIONS

Building on this discovery, I have found that people want to fulfill four basic purposes at some time in their lives. These purposes, then, motivate their actions, so I call them "purpose motivations." When they are practiced, they literally improve the quality of decisions you make about your job, as you will see in the next few pages. Mature people need to implement the following purposes in order to love their jobs:

- to serve
- to believe
- to recognize
- to act decisively and creatively

When individuals practice all four levels of purpose motivation at work or at home, they develop a committed attitude just as we saw it in the seventh attitude. Such people produce—responsibly, reliably, enthusiastically—over a lifetime.

Consequently, I believe Maslow's needs hierarchy works, but it doesn't tell the whole story. The other side of motivation is shown in Chart 2.

This set of motivations shows that you

can be a serving, believing, recognizing, creating person rather than a self-centered person. You can respond to your individual, creative purpose in life rather than be confined in what can become a prison of self-preoccupation.

You can begin to tap into the purpose motivations in your job by asking yourselve the following questions:

- How can I serve completely?
- What do I believe wholeheartedly?
- What is there to recognize immediately?
- How can I act more creatively and decisively?

Two Sides of Motivation

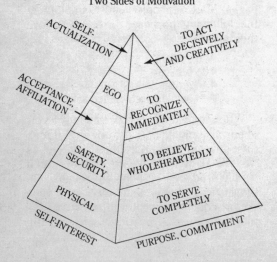

Chart 2

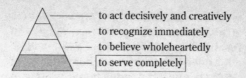

to act decisively and creatively

to recognize immediately

to believe wholeheartedly

to serve completely

SERVING COMPLETELY

In business, some organizations such as McDonald's have a corporate philosophy to serve, and they are growing at an astounding rate. "We do it all for you" sells billions of hamburgers. IBM was built on a belief that respect for the individual, service to the customer, and excellence in everything done is an inseparable combination. General Electric's statement, "We service what we sell," creates a responsiveness in customers.

Whether or not selfless motivation is sincere throughout an organization, service forms an essential part of our lives. An organization without a desire to serve is like a man without hands and feet, crippled in power to do what organizations must do if they wish to remain a part of our economy.

Great leaders recognize the importance of selflessness. The public hopes for it in their elected leaders. Military and religious leaders require it. But no one really understands it until he has tried it and found the tremendous motivation it gives to a job, a career, a relationship.

A middle-aged manager experienced it

when he took two months off work to stay at his sister's side in her final months of terminal illness. She had no family, and he felt a need to be there with her rather than letting her lie in a nursing home, waiting to die. While he did not intend it, his credibility as a total person on the job spread quietly from his location to other locations in his national business community.

My own experience in serving came years ago when a young couple and their son fled from communist Ethiopia and landed in America. They had nowhere to live, just the commitment of a church in Connecticut to find a place for them. I came home from the office and my wife said, "A refugee family has landed earlier than expected, and they need somewhere to stay for two weeks until the right place can be found."

"All right, we'll do it," I said.

On Saturday, the uncertain father, mother, and little son stood in our kitchen with gratitude and wonder showing on their brown faces. Goitom was a young, good-looking engineer. Senait was a beautiful ray of sunshine, and Biniam, a curly-haired, strikingly handsome boy.

We took a walk on our property later that morning. When I picked up Biniam to carry him across a stream, I felt a quietly powerful message inside, saying, in effect, "You are fitting into a larger purpose, and you must help." After six months of sharing our home, the family found a place to live. In that time, our lives had been enriched indescribably by responding to the powerful motivation to serve. To love your job, you must learn to serve completely.

WHAT ERODES SERVICE?

You and I need to experience the act of serving completely in our work. Our success in an organization depends on serving well. But how do we do that?

Service must go hand in hand with the seventh attitude, commitment, to be complete. The chart on the next two pages explains several kinds of service, both complete and incomplete. Look at it again before you go further. Two qualities—positive responsiveness (carrying out the intent and precise detail of a task when you have reason to believe it will work) and total initiative (doing something about all problems that you find)—are essential to serving completely.

Positive responsiveness. In some ways, you are like a commercial pilot who must make an instrument approach over an airport covered with heavy fog. Whether or not you are committed to responding to the messages you receive from your coworkers will cause the difference between success and failure, safety and catastrophe.

Total initiative. For an instrument landing to work, the air traffic controller must

Responsiveness

POSITIVE RESPONSIVE-NESS*	MALICIOUS OBEDIENCE	APATHETIC REACTION
Carrying out the intent and the precise detail, *when you believe it will work.*	Doing precisely what is directed, even if you know it won't work.	Uncaring performance of the letter of the command without consideration of the intent.

*Serving completely is practicing positive

offer total service, initiating conversation and responding to *all* the pilot's intent. The air traffic controller and the pilot share the common purpose of landing safely. Like them, you and your coworkers must be completely committed to one purpose to avoid disaster.

Self-serving. Ideally, when team members commit themselves to helping each other, they won't draw job boundaries designed to protect only one person. When someone says, "That's not my job," mark it as a signal of protectionism rather than teamwork. Protectionism, a primary form of self-serving, doesn't work in organizations any more than it does in an instrument landing at a fogged-over airport. Eventually teamwork erodes and total service drops off.

Malicious obedience. Another sure way to wreck service is to maliciously obey by

Initiative

TOTAL INITIATIVE*	SELF-SERVING	ORGANIZA-TIONAL SERVICE
Doing something about all problems that you find.	Initiating as well as responding, but only for your exclusive, personal gain.	Initiating and responding, but only to those in command and for mutual well-being.

responsiveness and total initiative at the same time.

doing your job to the letter and doing only what the manager says—especially when you know it won't work. For instance, a new manager says, "Let's invite the personnel directors to our advisory board." The subordinate says, "Sure," knowing all along that the personnel directors are paid to keep the organization out of trouble rather than provide creative innovations—knowing, too, that certain line managers or research people would add both a strategic and creative spark. That's malicious obedience.

Apathetic reaction. This is a result of the attitude of resignation you saw in chapter 2. It involves doing enough to get by, which ultimately contributes to dissatisfaction on your part and the part of your organization.

Organizational service. When you serve decisively and positively but lack a committed attitude, you render only organizational service. True leadership, job satisfaction, and the highest level of service come from commitment.

Our motivation deeply influences our service. A spirit of unwilling service spreads from one person to the next like the flu. Doing a job begrudgingly can never match total initiative, in which people start action and respond to all the team members in a common and constructive purpose.

☞ The Thirty-Day Motivation Plan

Here is a practical way to help put new motivation to work for you. Count thirty days on your calendar and write your objectives for that time. But in addition to your objectives, write on tomorrow's calendar date, *serve completely,* then, on the next day, *believe wholeheartedly.* Write *recognize immediately* on the third day and, on the fourth day, *act decisively.* By writing these words out—in any order you choose—on the succeeding days of the month, you will have increased the likelihood that you will do the things your own written words have said to do. Writing your resolve on thirty days of your calendar will help set your decisiveness in gear.

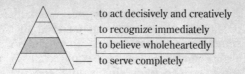

to act decisively and creatively
to recognize immediately
to believe wholeheartedly
to serve completely

BELIEVING WHOLEHEARTEDLY

For nine years I spoke at the American Management Association's premier management course in New York, San Francisco, Dallas, Chicago, Atlanta, and Toronto. In every city I asked middle-level managers to write down what they believed in when they thought of their own careers. For nine years, managers from all across the United States and Canada wrote what they believed in because people inherently know that behind their success lies a set of beliefs that has caused it, and they are willing to examine these beliefs as they look toward the future.

How does belief relate to your job and your happiness in it?

When you think of your organization or your product, what do you believe in? If you can't answer this question, you may need to find another organization or product—one that you can believe in. Because belief in your company can keep you coming back to it with your unique gifts, skills, and motivation.

Let's go deeper. When you think of your own strengths and aspirations at work, what do you believe in?

41

The entire astronaut program was built on finding astronauts who believed that someone could go around the moon. NASA also needed astronauts who could *believe in others* on the team that would support them. Further, NASA knew that when the orbit carried the astronauts around the back side of the moon, where no contact with earth was possible, the astronauts had to *believe in themselves* as the creators of success. If something went wrong, they had to believe they could fix it—alone.

If you can't believe in your gifts, you may need to sit down and write out the things that have made you a success in your past career. Draw a simple diagram on a sheet of paper that looks like Chart 3. Then fill in the three most significant successes you have had in each category and carry these into your future plans.

This is your personal pattern of success. You can believe in it because the pattern grew out of your past. Your pattern of success will be the best single predictor of success for you in the future.

THREE MAJOR SUCCESSES

School	Career	Leisure Time
1.		
2.		
3.		

Chart 3

100 PERCENT BELIEF

Believing wholeheartedly is the only way to get married, the only way to form a partnership, the only way to make a career change. Half belief or three-quarter belief or temporary belief just will not do. There is only room for wholehearted, sustaining belief. Without it, nothing gets done.

Wholehearted faith motivated people to build the Erie Canal for eight long years and 250 miles across New York State, even when they ran out of money. Sustaining belief drove the relentless railroad gangs as they worked their way across America from the east and the west, meeting at the golden spike in Utah. Behind every canal, railroad, bridge, and enterprise in America, there is belief.

Belief isn't past tense, it is *now*. Even as you read this, if you have faith in God's gifts to you, you have a spark of the same enthusiasm that created the bridges and railroads of America. The word *enthusiasm* is a spiritual word. It comes from *en* and *theos* and means "God within." Having faith that God is interested in what you do and, in fact, can be present in what you do can carry your motivation a step further.

Unless you have wholehearted belief in a purpose, in the possibility of *your* finding new purpose in your work, you need never start. But you *can* start, because belief is available to *you*—belief in your organization, your career, your strength, your potential. You can practice implementing your belief in the next thirty days and watch it grow.

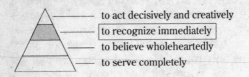

to act decisively and creatively
to recognize immediately
to believe wholeheartedly
to serve completely

RECOGNIZING IMMEDIATELY

Years ago, a secretary who worked for me didn't realize that she was judgmental of others in the department. Although she was attractive, bright, articulate, and competent, her attitude turned people off. When we talked about it, I asked, "Have you noticed some people aren't responding to your suggestions?"

"Yes," she said, "and I don't understand it."

"What you are telling them is correct. But it's the *way* you tell them that isn't working."

"What am I doing?" she asked, looking at me intently. She had moved from attention to interest. The next step was to find out if she wanted to fix it.

"I think you are standing on a pedestal, figuratively, and you are speaking down to your colleagues. Sometimes that means you show a touch of judgment in your manner or in the spirit of your advice. Often people can't detect a judgmental manner in our words alone—and neither can we—

but it happens anyway. For instance, it could be happening to me right now."

I looked at her carefully, reminding myself that I wanted to help her, not set her straight, and I wanted to remove any distance I might have caused. "Am I being helpful to you right now?"

"Yes," she said.

"For the next thirty days, would you like to have a little pact between us that may help?"

"Yes, I think so."

"All right, when I notice in a meeting or conversation that you are having with someone that they are getting turned off, I'll pull on my ear, like this. That will signal you that something just happened. I may not even know what happened, but at least we'll both know *something* happened. If you'll take note of what you've just said and your own motivation for saying it at that moment, we can talk about it later privately."

"Will you do that for me?" she asked, showing in her face that she appreciated the idea of our pact.

"I will, if you'll do the same for me."

"It's a deal," she said, with a big smile.

Years later, she came to me when she was a second-level manager and invited me to talk to her group about handling stressful relationships. Her way of speaking to others had been the single most limiting thing in her personal and career growth. Our agreement together to recognize something immediately turned out well.

THIRTY-DAY AGREEMENTS

For the next thirty days you can begin to experience an unusual power in your relationship to your job or, for that matter, any part of your life by entering into recognition agreements.

Recognizing immediately isn't just a nice thing to do, it's the powerful thing to do. When you agree in a pact with someone that you will give and receive honest feedback, you can learn how to improve your work and yourself. You can spot the reason things go well in yourself and others. Such an agreement helps you both.

A two-way agreement frees a person to repeat excellence. But what about recognizing poor performance?

When you see your colleague blow a presentation, the best time to recognize it is as soon as you can get the person alone and talk about it. But you may go about it in a right or a wrong way.

Here's an example: "Fred, I was watching what happened in your presentation, and I've got an idea that can help you next time. Are you interested?" If Fred isn't interested, maybe his ego has been too pounded for the moment and you can say, "Let's have lunch tomorrow, and I'll offer you a thought that can help." Or, if Fred says, "Tell me what went wrong," you can get in a quiet corner and say, "You're so comfortable with your topic that you wanted to pack everything in the twenty minutes you had, and you blew right by your audience. They were overwhelmed. Here's how much you could have covered, and they'd have been eager for a return presentation."

Either way, immediately recognizing success or failure helps you and the other person do better. But both of you have to agree not to provide feedback just to make you look good. When you recognize another's behavior, you need to aim at helping the other person get better, not at ego-boosting either yourself or him.

Did you ever run across someone who always wanted to tell you what you did wrong but never wanted to know from you how he or she did? The ability to see specifically what is going right or wrong is a two-way street. It works better when you both agree to give honest feedback immediately but with respect for the feelings of each other. This honest reflection becomes a helpful mirror for each, so that *both* of you will learn how to get better.

In your reflection, get at the cause of strength and the cause of weakness. Often those who give feedback use it as a tactic to make people like them, even though that's hard to admit; such a person usually doesn't even recognize that motivation. Deep down, everyone can appreciate real honesty if it's offered out of caring for their good. That way you both win.

HOW AGREEMENTS WORK

To recognize immediately and caringly frees up people to look at the cause of success or failure. By entering into a two-way agreement where each person supplies honest feedback, your skills get better and so does your relationship.

But your words must be honest and your manner must be caring. And it helps powerfully when you both focus on why you're doing something. That's real recognition. Aim not just at saying something nice, but aim at being helpful.

The freeing power of recognizing immediately becomes yours when you simply find a receptive colleague and say, "I've got something to improve that I'd like to work on, and I wonder if you will let me know when I'm missing the boat. If you'll do that for me for the next thirty days, I'll do the same for you."

You can try it for a month and watch it work. It works in the same way Weight Watchers works. Accountability to someone is a powerful motivation.

Serving completely, believing wholeheartedly, and recognizing immediately work better when you practice them at the same time. That way one purpose doesn't get overused and out of hand. But they are incomplete as sources of motivation until you follow the last step, acting decisively and creatively. The next chapter will show you how to do this.

Creative Decision Making

> *Next in importance to having good aim is to recognize when to pull the trigger.*—
> Elmer G. Leterman

In speaking on career planning across the United States and in foreign countries, I have found, much to my surprise, that most adults have left many of their career decisions to their companies or to someone else. Somehow they feel they get paid to make decisions for the company but not to make them for their future careers. As a result, they lose their energy and their organizations lose a powerful resource.

When I consulted for a senior vice-president of a major insurance corporation, I submitted a plan to help people in his company make decisions to increase their job satisfaction. We published a self-decision manual that was used successfully by both managers and nonmanagers. It began with a provocative statement adapted from an advertisement by a New York advertising firm.

This advertisement clearly indicates that to experience a new vitality at an old

☞ How to Retire at Thirty-five

It's easy. Thousands of people do it every year. In all walks of life.

And it sets our economy, our country, and the world back thousands of years in terms of wasted human resources. But worst of all is the personal tragedy that almost always results from "early retirement."

It usually begins with a tinge of boredom. Gradually a person's work begins to seem endlessly repetitious. The rat race hardly seems worth it anymore. It's at this point that many a thirty-five-year-old boy wonder or girl wonder retires. There are no testimonial dinners or gold watches.

He or she still goes to work every day, puts in forty hours, and even draws a paycheck. He or she has retired, but nobody knows it. Not at first, anyhow.

The lucky ones get fired in time to make a fresh start. Those less fortunate hang on for a while—even decades— waiting and wondering. Waiting for a raise or promotion that never comes, and wondering why.

job, you need to make some decisions about your career and your life in depth.

YOUR CAREER DECISIONS

On the surface, your career appears to be a series of jobs stretching over a lifetime.

There are always ways to fight back, though, and most people do. They counteract the urge to coast by running as they've never run before. They run until they get the second wind that is known as "self-renewal."

Self-renewal is nothing more or less than doing for yourself what your parents, teachers, coaches, and bosses did for you when you seemed young enough to need it. It's the highest form of self-discipline. And it can be one of the most satisfying experiences a person can enjoy.

Self-renewal is the adult's ability to motivate himself, to reawaken self-pride in the face of spiritual fatigue. Self-renewal is the device by which the boy wonders become men and girl wonders become women. They become leaders. Creators. Thinkers. Self-renewal is probably the greatest test a business person must face.

It's worth the effort, though. With life expectancy approaching the century mark, sixty-five years is a long time to spend in a rocking chair.

What can you glean from the jobs you have held and the one you now have to help you be happy in your current job or find a job better suited to you?

The way to a happier work life is to focus on your purpose and skills, both past and present, and to project them creatively into your future. You have brought some interests and skills into each job you have held and taken them from each job into the next. But if you haven't explored your individual purpose and refined your skills to carry it out—or if you haven't even focused on what your skills are—you have already accepted someone else's decisions on what your career ought to be. Your purpose and your skills together should be the basis for your decisions.

You can play a bigger role in your future job satisfaction by developing an idea of what you *should* be doing with your career and life now—no matter how long you've been working or how successful you are at the moment.

PERSONAL PURPOSE INVENTORY
As you have seen throughout this book, *you* are the key to a more productive and satisfying career in the future. But how do you get started?

Asking—and answering—"power" questions about your purpose can often help you discover what needs to change in your current circumstances. Select a person with whom you can discuss the following questions and set up a meeting for that purpose sometime within the next thirty days.

1. What purpose am I committed to as a person?

2. What is one thing I stand for and believe in?
3. What is my real strength at this point in my life?
4. Do I have a personal goal to achieve or a service that I want to perform in life—something that needs to be done or changed or eliminated? If so, what is it?
5. Am I interested in a specific job, either in or out of my organization, that requires skills I do not possess? If I am, what is it? What specific skills does the job require as I now view it?
6. Do I have one or more additional skills in mind that I want to develop? If so, what are they?

After you write out answers to the above questions, meet with your friend for advice. You can tell him or her what changes you would like to make, then commit yourself to taking the first step.

PERSONAL SKILLS INVENTORY
There are three types of skills in job performance: current job skills, portable job skills, and life or professional enhancement skills.

The list of examples in the chart on page 54 are only starters to help you recognize your skills. You can quickly list your skills right now on a sheet of paper for each of the following categories: (1) Known Skills (all the skills you now have); (2) Suspected

THREE TYPES OF SKILLS IN JOB PERFORMANCE

Current Job Skills	Portable Job Skills	Life Or Professional Enhancement Skills
Using office systems	Listening	Persuasiveness
Designing	Writing	Decisiveness
Researching, analyzing	Planning	Assertiveness
Coding	Speaking	Sensitivity
Assembling	Managing time	Self-control
Installing	Conducting meetings	Poise
Trouble shooting	Organizing	Use of humor
Repairing	Delegating	Initiative
Negotiating	Counseling	Commitment
Selling	Leading	
Buying	Developing	
Coordinating	Negotiating	

Chart 1

Skills (all the things you've wanted to be good at but haven't yet tried); (3) Known Weaknesses (areas of little interest or least skill).

Your skills generally will fall into four major areas: analytical-judgmental skills, technical-functional skills, relational skills, and creative-innovative skills. We'll discover more about these in chapter 5. You can rate yourself in these four areas of skill on the Job Approach Inventory in appendix 1. That is one way you can practice decisiveness and creativity right now.

Now that you have thought about your purpose and your skills, let's see how this fits into the four levels of purpose motivation we looked at in the last chapter. Consider the fourth level of purpose motivation: acting decisively and creatively.

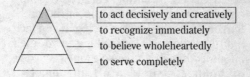

- to act decisively and creatively
- to recognize immediately
- to believe wholeheartedly
- to serve completely

WHY DO YOU WANT TO BE CREATIVE?

Chances are that you want to be creative and that you've always wanted to be creative. Remember when you built sand castles on the beach, played with blocks, dressed dolls, or colored beyond the lines in your coloring book many years ago? You were responding to a built-in urge to create.

Everyone wants to create something sometime. It's a desire built into us by the Author of life, and it's in everyone's blood from birth. For some it has been temporarily snuffed out. But it will return time and again. You want to create because you were made in the image of the Creator, God. All you need is encouragement and you will be creating again. Here are ten creativity-innovation tools to help you.

TEN TOOLS FOR GREATER CREATIVITY

One or more of these tools can work for you!

1. *Verbalized Issues, Challenges, and Problems.* Talking about something instead of just thinking about it actually changes your understanding of the problem or challenge you are facing. If you face a difficult decision, try talking to yourself about it while driving, use a tape recorder, or bounce your idea off an objective stranger. Your words will clarify ideas you thought you understood.

2. *Power Writing.* Writing an answer to a problem, even when you don't think you have an answer, often produces surprises. You know more than you think you know, especially where it concerns your wishes, dreams, or plans.

3. *Synergy.* Gather a group of people and agree to accept all answers or ideas without judging. This approach often engenders creativity, especially when each person is encouraged to build on the ideas of another.

4. *Power Questions.* Here are three power questions to use anywhere, in the middle of a meeting or alone at your desk:

- What is important?
- Why is it important?
- Who is important?

By asking these questions, you arrest your idea and drive it deeper. When you ask these questions of others, give them time to reflect on their answers by remaining silent. Ideally, they will respond to your silence with a new idea.

Five additional questions to apply to an idea are:

- Does someone need it?
- Is it simple enough?
- Is it compatible with human nature?
- Is it timely?
- Is it feasible?

5. *Force Field Analysis.* Getting things changed or accomplished is the process of overcoming an unseen force field. Often the reason things are the way they are is that there is a balance between barriers to achievement and enablers of achievement. Analyze what will enable and what will probably block your idea. Add more enablers to counterbalance the barriers.

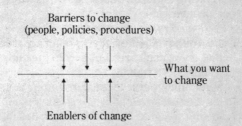

Barriers to change
(people, policies, procedures)

What you want
to change

Enablers of change

6. *Harnessing of Stray Ideas and Impulses.* Brilliant ideas are often lost or forgotten before they can be captured. When you see or hear an intriguing idea, decide

on the spot what you are going to do with it, even if it is as simple as calling someone else (see #1), writing down what you'd like to do with the idea (#2), or calling a meeting to explore it (#3).

7. *Multiple Hats.* By wearing more than one hat in life you increase your creative thought. Here are nine hats you can select from:

- intellectual product producer
- tangible program producer
- disciplined theorist
- software specialist
- professional leader (designer, builder, verifier, deliverer of products or services to meet any specification)
- trainer, coach
- consultant to users
- creativity catalyst
- entrepreneur

Wearing different hats increases your perspective.

8. *Perseverance.* Resolving to fight one more round is a key to winning a hard battle. If you can't see your way to the end, fight one more round.

Sometimes perseverance requires you to let your creative challenge go for a time, resolving to come back to it tomorrow. In the meantime, stay close to the problem but relax. The great inventor Thomas Edison used to bring a cot into his laboratory and sleep beside his problem. Submit your problem to your subconscious self while you sleep, or pray for extraordinary insight. You'll have fresh perspective when you return to it.

9. *Creative Use of Time.* No one has enough time, but everyone has the same amount in a twenty-four hour period. Using your travel time as creative thinking time and your waiting time as writing time can add to your effectiveness. Taking notes on what is happening around you can enhance your insight and your retentive powers.

10. *Creative Decision Making.* Making relevant decisions is the key. Everyone makes decisions, but the one who makes decisions that help people or the organization most is the one who profits most.

Four elements make a creative decision. You will recognize them!

- serving completely
- believing wholeheartedly
- recognizing immediately
- (then) acting creatively and decisively

Appendix 2 will help you examine each of these keys to creative decision making.

Creative decision making is a matter of practice, and there is no better place to practice than in the place you are now, in the job you now hold. Put on your consultant's hat and take a fresh look at your job. It has four rooms in it that you can creatively explore for potential places of growth. And that is what we will do in the next chapter.

Pushing Out the Walls of Your Job

Of course, we all have our limits, but how can you possibly find your boundaries unless you explore as far and as wide as you possibly can? I would rather fail in an attempt at something new and uncharted than safely succeed in a repeat of something I have done.—A. E. Hotchner

When I moved from upstate New York to the suburbs of Washington, D.C., I bought a house too big for my family. I had the feeling that someday my parents might need to move in with us in their retirement years. We had plenty of basement space off the recreation room, so I decided to make two additional rooms out of the empty basement space.

I wasn't a builder, but I knew what a hammer was. So one day I picked up my hammer, walked up to the recreation room wall where I thought a door ought to be, and bashed a hole in the wall. Two of my young sons, playing in the recreation room, momentarily looked stunned at my unusual act. One said in alarm, "Dad! What are you doing?" I picked up a saw and said, "This is the way you build a door, son."

I didn't really know how to build a door, but I didn't want my sons to think that! I broke out the wallboard to make the opening look like a doorway; then I stepped through the hole into the basement. Fortunately, the hole was between two two-by-fours.

When I went to the lumberyard, I discovered something called a prehung door. I had heard about prehung doors, but now I was ready to learn about one. I bought the door—hardware, knob, and everything all in place, and carried it down to the hole in the wall. Then I discovered why the lumber dealer told me to buy the shims, and I fit them around the new door to make it sturdy.

With twelve common nails, I hammered the door in place between the two-by-fours. I was delighted when it stood up. Then I put my hand on the knob, opened the door, and swung it. It clicked shut, just like a real door!

YOUR JOB: UNCOMPLETED ROOMS

Now my sons said in whispered amazement, "Dad can build a door!" I opened and shut that door five times or so, just feeling the excitement of my whole venture. Then I stepped through the door and built two complete rooms, not knowing anything about how to do it. I hung the dropped ceiling the lumber dealer sold me. It didn't look like a ceiling when it was delivered in little bundles of thin metal strips and packages of fiber tiles, but by the time I followed directions it did. Later, I laid tile on the floor, hammered sills for walls, and built two complete rooms. It took me two years (my wife said it took me three and a half), but I enjoyed it, because *I was growing while the rooms took shape.*

I found that I was no longer Don Osgood. I was Don Osgood plus two completed rooms. Nobody could ever take that experience from me. It made me realize that life is often a series of uncompleted rooms, just as jobs are.

Every job I've ever held had uncompleted rooms, and I've carried my hammer along with me into each job, quietly bashing a hole in each wall and finding that rooms that don't exist are built more easily than I thought they could be.

You can do the same.

Now that you've become aware of your attitudes and committed yourself to change, you can break out the walls of your job and build new ones. Doing this will give you new perspective, let you see the dimensions of your work as you've never seen them before, and allow you to do your job differently.

REDEFINING YOUR BOUNDARIES
When you bought your house or rented your apartment, you tried to notice

everything about your new place. For instance, you inspected the walls for quality, appearance, and feel. You asked yourself several questions. *Will this serve the purpose? Can I be comfortable? Is there anything I'm going to need to change here?* Your inquiring attitude brought discernment to your decision.

As we've seen, a constructive, questioning attitude at work opens the way for discovery. Using questions to locate and explore the boundaries of your job so you can redefine them is a powerful technique. Questions are the way you clarify your own expectations and the expectations of your management.

The walls of a room merely exist to carry out the purpose of the room, and that's the way a job should be. You can change the walls of your job—your job description—by putting the purpose or the desired end result of your job *first*. Here is a list of questions that will help you.

1. What is the mission or purpose of the organization I work in?
2. What is the purpose or end result of *this* job in the organization?
3. What am I trying to create?
4. What problems am I trying to resolve?
5. What specific steps are there in this job as it now exists?
6. What new steps are needed?
7. What steps should be removed?
8. How will I know when this job is done well?

9. What *self-interest motivation* is there in this assignment?
10. What *purpose motivation* is there in this job?

These ten questions can help you see not only what the job is but what it should be—and how it can become more productive. Asking them is the first step in pushing out the walls of your job.

In addition, most jobs have a mission or title that needs to be examined. You need to take the title to your job and make it your title, your mission. Does anyone else have ownership of this work? Is there a duplicate claim to the ownership of this job? Even if there are several other jobs like yours, your job is *your* job, simply because you are in it. Take charge. Look for the real purpose behind the job description.

When people see the purpose of their work, they will have purpose motivation. When people see the description of their job, they will have self-interest motivation. When people see the mission or the title of their responsibility, they will develop personal identification and ownership of their work.

JOB PURPOSE VS. JOB DESCRIPTION

I have made a remarkable personal discovery over the years. Most jobs can be changed in some way, often more easily than it seems, to make the work more valuable to the organization and more motivating to me. Further, when I have changed

64

my jobs over the years—redefined them and showed the way I felt they should be done—I automatically created more room to do them in. Then management became more inclined to leave me to do the work.

Take another look at the responsibility you hold right now. Somebody decided what the job should be two or perhaps even twenty years ago. In effect, the walls of your job were erected to solve a two-year or a twenty-year-old problem.

Whether you are an executive with people under you, a professional with people over you, or a person who works in virtual isolation, your job is now *yours,* however old it is. It is your opportunity and your responsibility to personally resist the idea that people should fit into job descriptions, as long as you can constructively replace that idea with this new one: *People should fit into job purpose, not into job description.*

Job description—what the work looks like—will flow out of job purpose. Job purposes seldom flow out of descriptions. Even if your old job description is still appropriate for today's job, you can improve it when you rebuild it on today's purpose.

THE FOUR ROOMS OF WORK
Let's look more closely at work in this way. Most jobs can be divided into four "rooms," or sections, which call for different activities. Many people work only on responsibilities of their job when they

could work in job "rooms" that allow new perspective, space, and growth.

Working in rooms rather than on tasks can keep people productive and motivated for years. The value of their work and their value as individuals increases measurably when they occupy more than one job room. The rooms of a job look like Chart 1.

THE FOUR ROOMS OR SECTIONS OF A JOB

I Analytical- Judgmental Responsibilities	II Technical- Functional Responsibilities
III Relational Responsibilities	IV Creative- Innovative Responsibilities

Chart 1

Chart 2 shows how a job looks when the purpose, rooms (or sections), and mission are well-defined.

Now that you are beginning to see that a job is more than a description, you can spend a moment thinking about what your job should be, not what it is. Use Chart 3 and write three to five specific responsibilities that fit into each room of your job. If you find it hard to list any responsibilities in one room, you have just discovered an area of your assignment that may need major reconstruction.

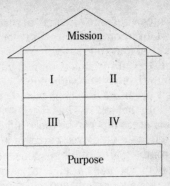

Chart 2

WHAT MY CURRENT JOB SHOULD BE

Area I: Analytical-Judgmental Responsibilities	Area II: Technical-Functional Responsibilities
Area III: Relational Responsibilities	Area IV: Creative-Innovative Responsibilities

Chart 3

If you can become effective in three out of the four rooms of your job—or even better, in all four rooms—you will be more valuable to your organization and yourself and you will enjoy your job more.

Often organizations neglect to see that every job that exists has four separate rooms or areas that can be more fully occupied. When an employee expands into another room or area of his responsibility or pushes out the walls of all four rooms, he will become more motivated and more productive *in the same job*. Following this approach, you will find the responsibility becomes bigger and makes more impact on the organization. This is good for everyone!

Sometimes a person pushes out the walls of a job so much that the roof threatens to fall in—in other words, he can't handle it. At this point management must decide whether the activities fit the mission of the job and the organization. If they do, yet the job has become too big, some of the less important responsibilities must be cut out or additional people must occupy the rooms and do the work. Each job depends upon the mission of the organization and on the worker's strengths, likes, and desire for growth.

Once you have decided that your job can become something more, that it has at least four rooms rather than a set of job tasks, you have the beginnings of new vitality at work. Here's how you can set about furnishing the rooms in your job.

MAKE A MENTAL CHANGE

First, create a new visual look in your job responsibilities. Begin by thinking about the four rooms in your job. What priority does each room have?

Now use Chart 4 on page 70 to draw the size of the four rooms according to the priority they take in your job. How much space should each room have?

Finally, imagine yourself in each of the four rooms of your job. Think not only about what *is* in the job but about what *should* be in the job, *if it is done with excellence*. It's like asking, "What furniture does this job room need?" or "How should the present furniture be rearranged?" To explore your job, try using the following questions:

- What is the real purpose of this job?
- What analytical-judgmental responsibilities are there?
- What technical or functional responsibilities are there?
- What relational responsibilities are there in this job, if it is done well?
- What creative-innovative responsibilities are there?
- What is the mission or title of this job?

Some jobs have more room for creativity and innovation than others. Some jobs have more relational opportunities than analytical potential. But all jobs have buried treasure in one or more rooms. Enter *all* the rooms, decide what tasks belong there, and start doing the tasks when you can. Just do them.

When you do this simple exercise, you will see your present job differently.

THE FOUR ROOMS OF MY JOB

Chart 4

MAKE A PHYSICAL CHANGE

Now look for some tangible way to let others know that you are bringing a new perspective to your job. Even if you have been in the job for a while, you can change the furniture, move the desk, hang a picture, do something different with your physical environment. Also, let your changes be a statement to yourself that you will approach your job differently.

I found a surprising difference in the reactions of people around me and an impact on my approach to my work when I moved my desk from the middle of my office to a wall. It opened up the floor space and allowed me to greet visitors without sitting behind the desk. A corner of my office became the area for desk work and another became the area for discussing ideas. Whenever I could, I even moved the phone so I had to get up to answer it. I looked for physical ways to change my approach to the job so that I would bring mental vitality to it.

Your office or work area need not be large, but it does need to be unique in some way as a visible reminder that you are occupying the space in a different way, with a new attitude.

ONE MAN'S STORY

Here's how one man, a trainer, began to make changes in his job. Chart 5 shows his approach to his job when he viewed it as having four sections, or rooms, of responsibilities rather than the responsibility of instruction alone. (If these sections or rooms of the job appear unusual, keep in mind that the job of a trainer, like any job, depends more on one's approach to it than on an initial statement of the responsibilities alone.)

FOUR ROOMS IN A TRAINER'S JOB

Area I: Planner (Analytical-Judgmental)	Area II: Administrator (Technical-Functional)
Area III: Instructor (Relational)	Area IV: Consultant (Creative-Innovative)

Chart 5

When you consider a trainer's job, you find that training doesn't involve just instructing someone in class. It includes planning the right things to instruct. It also requires consulting because the right things to instruct come from consulting with managers who want an organization problem solved or people to perform differently. The instructor must also create the right training at the right time for the right people. Finally, real instruction begins when the class is established and the student practices the skills the instructor teaches. The trainer's rooms now contain specific skills and tasks, as shown in Chart 6.

JOB TITLE OR MISSION
ORGANIZATION SKILLS DEVELOPER

Analytical-Judgmental Responsibilities (PROGRAM PLANNER)	*Technical-Functional Responsibilities* (ADMINISTRATOR)
• Defines training needs • Sets course objectives • Picks training methods • Uses appropriate education programs • Measures program effectiveness	• Develops overall program strategy • Secures financial and physical resources • Schedules and publicizes programs • Enrolls students and speakers
Relational Responsibilities (INSTRUCTOR)	*Creative-Inovative Responsibilities* (CONSULTANT)
• Conducts classroom activities to meet program objectives • Conveys and interprets information and concepts to students • Responds flexibly to class needs • Leads classes in learning	• Responds to requests for help from management • Helps to identify problems and finds solutions • Creates new education programs • Initiates recommendations to management

JOB PURPOSE: Determine what the organization needs to have done and teach employees to do it, more efficiently and productively, for the mutual benefit of the organization and the individual.

Chart 6

After looking at the rooms, the trainer realized his job is more suitably titled "organization skills developer" rather than "trainer." You, too, may discover a new purpose in your job after you've "furnished your rooms"!

CREATING NEW ROOMS

What happens if you run into a wall? What do you do when there doesn't seem to be any opportunity for new types of responsibilities?

That becomes a matter of honest negotiation. How you negotiate the construction of new rooms with your manager—especially when he or she put the walls in place—is our next topic. Because relationships are as important as walls, you've got to treat managers as though they were your customers, as you will see in the next chapter.

Convincing Your Manager

The most important single ingredient in the formula of success is knowing how to get along with people.—Theodore Roosevelt

Treating your manager as your customer will make all the difference in how open your manager will be to a change in your job. What you think of as constructive may be perceived by him or her as destructive. No one wants to change a room in a house if it will destroy the value of that house.

YOUR MANAGER AS CUSTOMER

It doesn't matter who you are, how high your level in management or non-management, or how secure you have felt in the past, you will be afraid of change if it seems to put your comfort and security— the rooms in your job or your career—at stake. When someone comes to you with a new idea that will change your responsibility, reputation, or place in your organization, you will need special insight, confidence, and flexibility to greet the new idea warmly rather than suspiciously. That's because under every suspicion lies fear. Under all fear there is a lack of confidence.

When someone wants to change your organization, *you* are at stake, not just your job or your organization. This feeling of personally being at stake applies to everyone in management, from the chairman of the board all the way down to the beginning manager. Contrary to the beliefs of people far down in the organization, the chairman of the board can become just as insecure as the newest employee. He just shows it differently. When the chairman becomes afraid, he uses his leverage to make sure things don't change or that they change quickly. That is why your manager, regardless of level, should be treated in a considerate way.

All managers are customers. They deserve to be treated as you would treat your *best* customer, no matter how good or bad your manager is. More important, *you* deserve to treat your manager as your best customer, because your approach is the key to seeing your organizational relationships become more successful than you've ever seen them before. The tremendous power of relationship becomes yours when you develop the attitude in all your dealings that *everyone you meet is your customer.*

HOW TO TREAT CUSTOMERS

Experienced salespeople know that a customer isn't just someone to be sold on a preset idea of theirs unless it is something the person really can use and benefit from. There are few farmers' daughters anymore, and most of them have been around long enough to have become sophisticated city people. Today's customer looks for solutions to problems, whether the customer is a woman, man, the chairman of the board, your manager, or a colleague.

When you find yourself frustrated with a problem and you finally work your way around to doing something about it—when you reach the decisive attitude—ask yourself: *Since this is my manager's problem, too, how can I solve this from his perspective?*

Then think of the impact on everyone else involved. If you want to change the rooms in your job, show why the change will work for all concerned.

Finally, propose a trial period—thirty days, perhaps—that allows an opportunity for your idea to be implemented without a commitment to change the organization forever. Sometimes that kind of commitment appears too unsettling to an organization.

When I started the New Perspectives program for experienced IBM employees, I announced to the marketing regions across the United States that I merely wanted to experiment with a new program.

I would run only three classes before deciding whether to continue. From the start I made it clear that the program would be voluntary. After the first class of thirteen people, little doubt remained that we had struck on something worthwhile. Three classes later, the idea had sold itself, and the program continued for many years, even after I had left IBM.

When you approach your manager or your peers as though they are your customers and say, "I've got something that I'm quite sure will help me and other employees stay alive and vital on the job," you've already got the attention of anyone who thinks he may have a potential problem. But now you've got to close the sale.

CLOSING THE SALE

Let's revisit an old idea for treating people as customers. It's the AIDA approach—a simple but sound sales approach that works with anybody, managers included.

The AIDA Approach

A	Attention
I	Interest
D	Desire
A	Action

When you want to try something new or get someone else to try something new, you've got to get the attention of the person. First, you've got to ask some searching questions. *What will most likely get my customer's attention?* Once you've got his or her attention, ask, *What will be of most interest? Is it organization savings, speed, or quality, or is it self-interest or some purpose the person has?* Next ask, *What would this person really want?*

Remember, desire is one of the factors that changes a person's attitude. If you don't know what the person wants and you can't figure it out, ask. Honest questions make it unnecessary to spend too much time or money on market research and, as we have learned, the right questions can cause powerful change—especially when you have a workable idea. Actually, questions *are* market research.

With the New Perspectives program, I just said in effect, "Here's what I'd like to do." I told them I had reserved our Sands Point facility, the most prestigious conference center in the corporation. That was the attention step.

Then I said, "I guarantee you a bell-ringer program that no one will be forced to support in the future. We won't even continue it unless it turns out to be valuable." That was the interest step.

Next I asked a simple question. "Would you like to send someone?" That was the desire step. No mystery, no manipulation, just a question—*after* the attention and the interest steps had been taken.

I offered sixteen vacancies and ended

with thirteen participants. That was the action step.

Later, when the program had already proven itself in the first three classes, I invited the vice-president of the division to speak. I approached him as though he were a customer. "I've got something you ought to see," I said. After his first visit, he spoke in virtually every program I held, sometimes taking red-eye flights from the West Coast to make it to the class on time.

Attention, interest, desire, and action: This time-tested, honest, practical way works when you use it to approach anyone about anything. The trouble is, most people forget to use the approach with their own managers. Instead of treating managers as clients, employees approach them with a problem or a complaint, creating distance at just the time they need to reduce distance.

You can effectively deal with people above you by following this rule: *Never bring a problem to your manager without a proposal.* This works only for those who know a powerful truth: *All problems are proposals in disguise.* How do you turn a problem into a proposal? By thinking of the problem as a way to get attention, followed immediately by an intriguing idea to solve it, followed immediately by a question to determine desire, followed by a clear-cut statement of the next step you propose. But none of this should be done in a conversation alone.

USING VISUAL IMPACT

The value of visual impact increases the
likelihood of agreement, just as turbodrive
increases the power of a little engine. In an
organization, for a good little idea to make
a far-reaching impact, it only takes the
right approach when you bring the concept to the people who have the power to
decide what to do with it. Consider this for
a moment.

We retain:
10 percent of what we read
20 percent of what we hear
30 percent of what we see
50 percent of what we hear and see
70 percent of what we say
90 percent of what we say and do

These figures may vary by individual
and circumstance, but they show an important principle when dealing with a good
idea. *Never let a good idea down with an
ineffective approach.*

Many years ago I had a manager who wanted me to present instructional material his way. I tried, but I had difficulty, and I couldn't get him to listen to me. Finally, I wrote him a letter. Instead of sending it, I brought it to him so he could read it while I stayed with him and we could talk about it. He asked, "Why did you send me a letter when you could have just told me?"

"I *did* tell you, but my message wasn't coming through; so I thought it would help if you could see what I was saying while you hear me say it to you." All my prior discussions did not compare to this one approach. The approach paved the way for me to say, "I owe it to you to achieve the objectives of this job, and I'm committed to do that. But since I have difficulties doing the job your way, you owe it to me to let me do it a different way." Our communication was more effective from that time on, and our relationship moved from frustration to deeper awareness and years of mutual appreciation.

Years later, along with another manager, I met with a hand-selected group of professional educators to determine how to build a new management development program. IBM's management development had been well in place for years, including our requirement for every manager to take forty hours of management training every year. But now we faced the task of making succeeding years of training even more relevant than preceding years. It was not an easy task, and none of us knew how to do it.

We had embarked on a program of skill training rather than awareness training alone, and I held the role of architect of a series of skill workshops for our managers around the world. The first meeting of our advisory board was held at a hotel in Florida, overlooking the ocean. We picked the location to signal to the participants that we sought new vision and new depth of vitality in management education. We treated our board as customers.

I had gone to the best visual artist I could find and had him draw a picture of the world with a series of nine skill workshops rising out of the ocean, which would meet the needs of managers for technical-functional skills, analytical-judgmental skills, creative-innovative skills, and relational skills. I had him draw twenty transparencies of this and other ideas that my colleagues and I felt might produce a "world-class manager."

We later settled on the "excellent manager" as a more suitable title to use, and out of our effort came IBM's International Management Skill Series. But the vision caught on because we let our advisory board *see* it rather than just talk about it. We turned a problem into a proposal, and we made sure that everyone *saw* the vision while they *heard* about it—and we made sure they talked about what the vision really had to become in order to be successful.

We had no difficulty selling IBM on the idea. They were just waiting for a proposal, having already decided that management development would continue as a key to the future.

I learned, as you will, to treat everyone as my customer, including management above and people below. I learned that obtaining attention, interest, desire, and action is a good way to deal with people around you, especially when you are looking for a whole new approach that will affect the entire organization (or the entire nation, if that is your interest).

WHEN YOUR MANAGER WON'T BITE

But what if you can't convince your manager?

You can always get the objectives of your job done so that anyone who looks on can see that they are done, and you can perform the job as it is now described. But at the same time you can do the creative things that you've discovered make the job really work for you. Just do them. If time shows that they work better, let your performance speak for itself, and you'll automatically receive more room to work out your job even more creatively.

In other words, you can make your job more enjoyable even without a formal change in it, just as the train conductor I mentioned in chapter 1. The key is to take charge just as a person named Truman did when he became the president of the United States. Be the president of your job and your career. And if that doesn't work, you can look for the right opportunity to move on to another job.

In the meantime, you can draw on the unlimited power of the Creator of the universe in whose image you are created. You can achieve the attitudes you need. You can serve beyond the ability of others to serve. When asked for your shirt, you can give your coat, too; a concept that has helped revolutionize the world.

You can believe wholeheartedly in the gift of extraordinary creative power within. You can learn to recognize immediately what is causing success or failure and make the changes that are needed. You can act decisively and creatively by changing the internal walls in your job and by moving the furniture around. You literally can live a decisive, creative life because you are not alone.

You have a Presence always available to you, one that I have tapped into through this on-the-job prayer, which I have breathed in a silent moment in the middle of a routine meeting or in a major crisis:

> Lord, I need your attention now.
> Give me your creative heart,
> Your mind of wisdom,
> Your spirit of discernment,

So that I can serve your purposes
Where I am now
In this moment.

With that request you can begin to realize that you are not alone. You never were, and you never will be.

Job Approach Inventory

Here are four skill areas that will affect your job and career success:

I. Analytical-Judgmental
II. Technical-Functional
III. Relational
IV. Creative-Innovative

Each area has several specific characteristics. Look at the characteristics listed on the following pages, and rate yourself on each one using the scale provided.

I. Analytical-Judgmental

Problem Identification
- I probe for key information on matters that I am not familiar with.
- I organize information from a variety of sources to find solutions to problems.
- I identify the subtle relationships between facts.
- I look for inconsistencies in information.

Judgment
- I select what is important from a volume of information.
- I pick the key items to spend my time on.
- I know when to support and when to challenge others.

Decision Making
- I consider consequences before making my decisions.
- I realistically access what can be done and when.
- I involve others in decisions affecting them.

	ALWAYS	OFTEN	SOMETIMES	SELDOM	NEVER

II. Technical-Functional

Organizational Awareness

- I keep in touch with what's going on across the organization.
- I anticipate new demands for services and products.
- I develop plans and goals that carry out organizational and individual objectives.

Administrative Controls

- I create or innovate procedures to evaluate alternatives and to accomplish tasks.
- I document important details of decisions and actions.
- I maintain up-to-date and reliable records about activities and resources.
- I incorporate promising ideas even without complete data.

ALWAYS	OFTEN	SOMETIMES	SELDOM	NEVER

III. Relational

Interpersonal

	ALWAYS	OFTEN	SOMETIMES	SELDOM	NEVER
• I look for what others mean beyond what they say.					
• I give explanations for my request.					
• I tailor my approach to the needs and goals of others.					
• I maintain objectivity even in tense circumstances.					
• I deal with conflict in an honest and straightforward manner.					

Oral Communication

- I present material in a helpful and understandable way.
- I adapt my communication approach to the needs and experience of the audience.
- I make effective presentations when needed.

Written Communication

- I absorb and understand written material quickly.
- I express ideas clearly and persuasively in writing.

	ALWAYS	OFTEN	SOMETIMES	SELDOM	NEVER

IV. Creative-Innovative
   Change Anticipation
   - I see the need for change well ahead of time.
   - I revise my approach to meet changes in circumstances and resources.
   - I present and receive bad news honestly.

   Problem Solving
   - I deal confidently with hard-to-define problems.
   - I use my past experience and experience of others.
   - I press for solutions even when I can't get complete information.

   Utilization of Ideas and Resources
   - I deal with ideas as well as details.
   - I adapt useful information regardless of the source.
   - I incorporate promising ideas even without complete data.

Select the three to five specific characteristics in which you are most proficient and list them here:

List the three to five lowest here:

Four Keys to Creative Decision Making

SERVING COMPLETELY
- Who am I serving by this decision? Just me? Or am I serving my manager, supervisor, customer, or company?
- Am I providing in this decision the kind of service that will make an extraordinary difference? Will this take care of someone's needs? Will someone use what I am providing?

BELIEVING WHOLEHEARTEDLY
- Can I believe in the result of this decision? Will others believe in it? Why?
- Does this decision tap a profound motivation of people?
- Will I be able to live with the result, be enthusiastic about it, and support it over time?

RECOGNIZING IMMEDIATELY
- Have I recognized the creative tools that will improve this decision?
- Have I considered what is making

things go well and what is making things go wrong?
- Have I talked about this decision with the right people?

ACTING CREATIVELY AND DECISIVELY
- When must I decide?
- When will it be too late?
- Have I considered the three steps above before deciding?
- Has that consideration changed this decision for the better?

About the Author

As president of the Career Performance Group, DON OSGOOD runs New Perspectives, a unique leadership development program designed to create vitality and productivity in the workplace. Don's customers range from professional associations to Fortune 500 companies including IBM, International Paper, and The DuPont Company.

Don is also an author and a motivational speaker. His books include *Fatherbond* and *Surefire Ways to Beat Stress* (Tyndale). He has spoken to corporate and professional organizations across the United States and in Europe, Latin America, and the Orient.

Previously, Don was a program manager at IBM's corporate-wide Management Development Center. He held managerial and staff assignments in six major operating units in his thirty years at IBM.

Don serves on the boards of Houghton College and the Christian Herald Associations. He and his wife, Joan, live in Pound Ridge, New York.

POCKET GUIDES
ALSO FROM TYNDALE